BEAUTIFUL ROA

Other books of White Eagle's Teaching

BEAUTIFUL
ROAD HOME

WHITE EAGLE

LIVING IN THE KNOWLEDGE
THAT YOU ARE SPIRIT

THE WHITE EAGLE PUBLISHING TRUST
NEW LANDS · LISS · HAMPSHIRE · ENGLAND

First published July 1992
Second impression April 1997

© Text and illustrations copyright
The White Eagle Publishing Trust, 1992

British Library Cataloguing-in-Publication Data
A catalogue record for this book is
available from the British Library

ISBN 0-85487-088-1

Set in 12 on 15pt Sabon and
printed in Great Britain at
the University Press, Cambridge

CONTENTS

PREFACE

The title and the theme of this book might suggest a slight change in presentation from many of the volumes of White Eagle's talks that have been issued in the last few years. The idea for it grew from a shared inner awareness among those of us responsible for putting his teaching into print, that he wished us to make clear what is perhaps the keynote of his teaching, namely that spirit *is* life—*not just a different world, but the reality of life itself. The everyday consciousness we have is of a dimmed world, sometimes joyful and frequently painful. White Eagle would say that it is within our own awareness that the secret of happiness lies: that the more we realize that existence is love, not limitation, the more we release ourselves into a true and joyful awareness wherein the experiences of the everyday world have meaning and beauty.*

During the editing required to make the book into coherent chapters, it became clear how often in the extracts chosen White Eagle referred to the Creation story in the book of Genesis, the story of Adam and Eve. Those who read the book will see that he repeatedly describes life as a great cycle, in which man–woman leaves the eternal consciousness, the 'heaven world', to seek the growth-experience of seeming to be separate from God, and returns at last to God with greater wisdom; or, shall we say, having through the very act of incarnation been part of the ever-expanding love of God.

'Beautiful Road Home', a title which had already come to us as one which conveyed a special message from spirit, thus describes the journey that every woman and every man is taking: a journey in which a veil is slowly lifted from his or her eyes, to reveal a path of infinite beauty and light. We pray that it will be a helpful message.

All the books of White Eagle's teaching are, in one way or another, comprised of extracts from talks he has given through the mediumship of Grace Cooke at group meetings and services over many years, and its publication quietly marks the centenary of her birth. In the case of the present book, all those teachings except the final one and one addressed to an evening audience of young people are Sunday addresses to a general audience or congregation; and really the message that we have felt urged to pass on today is the one that White Eagle has been putting forth for over fifty years. We hope that emphasized as it is in this book it will come to the reader with a particular strength. Some of the chapters are complete teachings, others are extracts carefully put together in a way that provides continuity within the book's message. Those with a particularly sensitive ear will recognize a short passage which also appears in THE QUIET MIND, here in its fuller context. Because the book is compiled from separate teachings it can sometimes be helpful to read a chapter or a passage at random. Let the book speak to you; it *does not require of you that you read it from cover to cover!*

In the teachings as he gave them (for some were given quite early in those fifty years of work), White Eagle followed normal usage and regularly used the word 'man' in an abstract sense, inclusive of both sexes. Even in such a short passage of time, the word is already much less easily read in that inclusive sense than it once was. We have altered it to specify both man and woman, where this can be done without destroying its abstract sense and making it more personal than we believe White Eagle intended. In respect of the word 'brotherhood', in many cases it actually expresses a quality of being, and this sense is carried over into the word when used here to denote a group of people, both male and female. In this case it has been thought better to leave the word unaltered, thereby acknowledging the changing quality of our language, and allowing the reader freedom to understand White Eagle's teaching in its spirit, rather than its letter.

We would like to acknowledge and thank the unknown artist of the little drawings in our text, which were simply found among our archives. We have added them because we felt they conveyed the happiness of the world that White Eagle, in this book, wishes to describe for all of us.

In common with our normal style the quoted words of Jesus are italicized in the text.

JCH
June 1992

ix

CHAPTER I

THE KINGDOM OF EARTH AND
THE KINGDOM OF HEAVEN

Within every man and woman is the capacity to become aware of the worlds invisible, intangible, because this is the truth of their being. *Every* man and woman can be touched and awakened to those higher worlds, some in small degree, others greater. But in the course of growth, all will learn to open the windows of this house of clay, and see the glorious panorama; they will become aware, even while living on earth, of that heavenly world which is their true home.

The earth is not home, it is just a place you visit in order to be educated. On earth you may journey over the ocean to visit other lands, both for pleasure and education, or perhaps to give service to the community in some form or another. So the journey of your soul into incarnation is but another journey to a foreign land.

We understand how difficult it is for you, living in the midst of turmoil and materialism, to appreciate the truth of the life of the spirit, or to realize your true home. Do not look upon heaven as a place to which you will journey, for the first time perhaps, after the death of your physical body. Cultivate here and now the idea that the world invisible is your true home. There is that within your breast which intuitively longs for heaven, and which receives spiritual inspiration. Your spirit contacts and knows truth; it speaks to you when you enter the silence, the stillness of your innermost heart, or perhaps after you have passed through some great emotional stress—or when sorrow has shaken your soul to its foundations.

The still small voice of the spirit, or of your master, speaks first in the quiet sanctuary of the heart, calling you to withdraw from the materialism of everyday life.... The master calls *you* up the mountain-side as Jesus called his disciples. The voice calls in various ways, but always it calls you nearer to your true home.

Few people in these enlightened days believe in the story of the Garden of Eden. When the intellect analyzes and dissects the teaching of the bible, it cannot accept the words it reads at their face value. 'It is an affront on man's intelligence!' the person says today. Then science comes along and makes a clean sweep of all the ancient teachings within it, and in doing so casts aside the growing corn which might have been the bread of heaven to man.

But humanity may yet retrace its steps to belief in that ancient myth, for it tells the story of how man, at one time, dwelt in a home of peace and plenty, of joy and happiness, an innocent child of God, with no knowledge of what lay outside Eden. Once, however, Adam and Eve had tasted the fruit of the Tree of Knowledge, they knew there were many things to learn. By their own choice they tasted that fruit, and so were sent forth from the Garden, which with their new knowledge had ceased to be heaven to them; their spirit knew that it must leave the 'Garden of Eden' to gain experience and more knowledge, and to use what it had already learned.

We are told that Adam and Eve were driven out of heaven. They left the home of God their Father and, rather as in the parable of the prodigal son, journeyed forth into the world, there to earn not only the bread to feed the body, but the bread to feed the mind, the soul, the spirit. Humankind has been on this journey ever since, gaining experience and learning through joy and sorrow, pain and suffering, to grow wise.

When Adam and Eve left the Garden of Eden, an angel with a flaming sword guarded the gate, and they could not return. A soul cannot pass through that gate into the heavenly places until it has learned the password. The password is composed of certain letters; you are all learning to pronounce, or to sound these letters as you learn the necessary lessons of life. Every lesson perfectly learned by you is a 'letter' of

13

this password, a 'letter' not spoken by the lips, but *lived in the life*. A soul must journey forth to strange lands again and again in order to learn the password which, when sounded in the ether, will cause those flaming swords to be withdrawn, and the gates of heaven to fly open to it forever.

We have long worked from our side of life to stimulate man's spirit and to awaken the spiritual consciousness within human souls. At the present time humanity is wavering between two paths—the path of sheer materialism which will only lead it to greater darkness and deeper misery, and the other path which leads upwards to a more beautiful life for man–woman, not only while in the world, but when they journey onward into the blessed land of light and love. Many people still think, we suggest erroneously, that when they die they will sleep awaiting the sounding of a last trumpet. Other people believe that life in the spirit world is a life of slothful ease where every desire is satisfied; this also is untrue. *Life means work!* Man will begin to find the true meaning of life when he recognizes this truth. Yet although life means work it does not mean that it need be toilsome and wearying work. No, it means that life is full of interest, full of activity, full of service.

Jesus said, *Be ye perfect even as your Father which is in heaven is perfect*. Earthly-minded people say this is impossible in an imperfect world. But then, who made the world imperfect? All God's creation in the nature kingdom is beautiful. All God's creatures in the animal and human kingdom would be as beautiful if man would obey the laws of God. Instead, people break God's laws every moment they live, and the result is chaos, suffering, pain and sorrow. In other words, man–woman has been given freewill, the highest gift that God could bestow upon His sons and daughters, who have chosen to respond to the vibrations of their lower nature, to those of darkness instead of light.

My brothers and sisters, do not despair; do not think it impossible in a material world for the light of God to manifest through the human being. The whole purpose of creation is for divine love to shine forth from within, outwardly; and every soul which has been breathed forth from the heart of beloved Father–Mother God will eventually manifest, through the flesh, all the divine attributes. This has been exemplified for you in the life, in the teachings and in the works of the great masters, and, above all, in the Christ; who said, *The works that I do, shall he do also; and greater works than these shall he do.* The world still doubts, is still unable to understand these teachings. All manner of excuses are made. The great intellects of the day turn and twist the Master's words until they lose the simple power and strength of the spirit. We say that the words spoken by Christ are true in every particular. God is not some being far removed from humankind. Do you not see that God is nearer than breathing, closer than hands and feet?

What do these words mean? They mean that God, the divine fire of life, rests within the heart of every living soul, like a seed. Many layers are covering this seed of the divine spirit. But God has given you freewill to enable you to nurture this seed and to make it grow. In the winter the flowers of spring were only little brown bulbs. You could hold a bulb in your hand and marvel that within it there rested a beautiful flower which would in due season come forth, perfect and beautiful in shape and colour and perfume. What a miracle has arisen from that little brown house! You, my friends, are like that little brown bulb; you

have a like treasure within your heart. You can, if you will, put forth an effort which will cause the radiant flower of the spirit within you to grow—quietly, imperceptibly at first; but in due season its flowering will be so strong that your body will take its form, meaning by this that your body will become as perfect as the divine man–woman. Only you have it in your power to bring about this perfection. You worship God as your Creator, but God has given to you the power within to create whatever you will.

You have all helped to create your present world. You have also helped to create your own body. During every new incarnation you inherit the conditions you have sown in your past. Even now you are

16

creating the condition in which you live. You will say, 'Oh, but I did not choose my kind of work, I did not choose the conditions I find so uncongenial'. Make no mistake, my brother, my sister. Your present life is of your own creation.

Once you can really accept that fact with courage and with sweet surrender to the wisdom and love of God, you can set about developing the divine within you, creating on a higher level, on a higher vibration, a life which is harmonious, beautiful and happy.

Earth life is the greatest opportunity given to God's children to gain experience. It is indeed true that the soul passes through wonderful experiences after death, yet there is no state of life that provides finer opportunities for development and growth of the soul than the physical—than incarnation on earth. This is why we say that every effort should be made to perfect life, and to extract from life the honey of the flower which God has caused to be created on earth. Your real life, your experience and your destiny in every incarnation, is to grow towards God-consciousness, which you will do by learning to love your fellows.

Love one another, said Jesus. But no; it seems the soul must struggle for itself, and say: 'If I do not look after myself, no-one will look after me'—forgetting the cosmic law, which is Love, the law from which all creation is built and sustained. The angels weep over the turmoil and inharmony caused through man's

17

lack of understanding and lack of love for his brother man. But everyone in your country and in the world today who knows the truth can do more than they can ever realize, by standing firm in their resolve to let the law of love rule every part of their lives. We say because we know it is true, 'Good shall come out of evil, light shall come out of darkness.' There is a light hidden in the heart of the dark cave and it will rise and blaze forth. Lazarus was asleep in the dark cave of death until Jesus said, *Lazarus come forth!* And Lazarus arose, he left the grave-clothes of his materiality and foolishness. He came forth at the command of his Lord, a changed man.

The outcome of darkness is light, goodness and progress—look for it. But you yourselves, every one of you, must play your part. You do not understand the power of thought or the power of prayer. Don't be miserable; don't get depressed and cry, 'All is lost! What is man coming to?' My children, man is coming to God, in God's way! A new golden age will come, when all shall turn their faces towards the golden Sun, the Christ. Their hearts shall be filled with joy, their feet shall dance, and their voices shall be raised in thanksgiving and praise for the gift of life from their Creator, the Great Spirit.

CHAPTER II

MAN AS CREATOR

God created you to know the happiness which souls in heavenly places know. When the soul is released for a time from its mortal body and it aspires to truth in God in the heavens, that soul casts away its earthiness and in time ascends to planes of beauty and happiness. You may be thinking, 'Well, if the soul ascends to happiness, why does it ever return again to this earth?' We will tell you. The soul returns to continue its lessons so that it can, in time, so perfect itself that it is able to bring all the divine attributes into manifestation on earth. How can the kingdom come until you, until all humankind, has learnt how to create heaven on earth? And this you will do.

When the will to become Christlike grows strong in the heart, it causes an opening in the consciousness for the greater self to descend into the physical body. You are not here on earth. You think you are? You think that your physical body is *you*, but it is only an infinitesimal part of you. If you would contact your true self, go into a place of quiet to commune with your Creator in your heart. Then you will rise in consciousness. That great light to which you rise is, you will find, the divine man—you, yourself, your own divinity, the real you. By opening your consciousness to this divine self your whole vibrations will be raised and your body become purified.

You are a son–daughter of the living God. In great love He bore you, or They bore you, brought you into an incarnation. And although you meet suffering and trial, and maybe life is very hard for you at times, nevertheless, you will find that underneath all this turmoil and heartache there is a power carrying you along. You may have to endure accidents, illness, bereavement, poverty and all manner of suffering through man's inhumanity to man, but if you are honest with yourself as you look at your life, you will admit that in a miraculous way you have been helped, you have been guided, you have been brought through your trials and difficulties. So it will be to the end of this particular physical life, if you can only resign yourselves to that love of which Jesus continually spoke in his simple teaching to his disciples and to the multitude.

Within your heart is a seed, placed there by God, which is the seed-atom of life; and when you understand the law, when you are operating the law, this seed in your heart can put you in direct touch with that all-embracing Light of life. When we speak of the seed, we refer not to the soul, but to the pure spirit. The soul is the garment of the spirit, the etheric body which is the individual's link between heaven and earth. The soul receives impressions from the creative sphere of pure light and transmits these impressions to the human brain. And man with the love in his heart, the light within his heart, will use that power to create beauty—he will create in sound, he will create in colour, he will create in form, he will create in language, he will create within in his own life. All people have within them this power to create, which is illumined, quickened, by that pure white light, Spirit. And spirit is all love. This is why, until a man or woman loves, and understands what love is, he or she is unable to create perfectly. Perfection comes only through that pure Christ love. And this love, which we have described to you many times as light, is the power which causes the seed-atom in the heart to grow.

As it starts to grow in you, don't stifle it: encourage this feeling of love, of tolerance, of goodwill. Encourage it, because as you do so you are growing in spiritual power and wisdom. If you could see clairvoyantly you would know that in that little seed there was a spark of life, and this life would appear to you as light. You would see that little seed as a fire.

In ancient times the priests would create fire on the altar from seemingly nothing. The priest would place his hands in a certain way, and say certain words, and there would come the little light and then gradually the fire, and the fire would grow to a great blaze—a demonstration to our people of the life of God, which came out of space, out of silence, into manifestation in physical form.

We see the white light shining through the little seed and drawing it up from the darkness towards the sun, until it breaks its bonds, helped by the sunlight, and is transformed out of a tiny seed into the green corn, or a perfect flower. This again is a demonstration to humanity of the existence of an invisible power, a life which is in the ether all round men—but most of all in the human being itself.

We hear the question, 'Why then do I have to suffer—I suppose it is my karma? Whose karma is it when there is national suffering, international suffering?' We answer the question thus: it is humanity's karma. Remember, you are all as yet children. Many of you are in the kindergarten. Some of you have passed into higher standards, and a few have graduated into the university of spiritual science. Those who have learnt to live in accord with the law of love and brotherhood are not only helping themselves, but helping to release the whole of humankind from the bondage of its karma. This is how good is done—not by rushing about and fighting or shouting and talking. When man and woman become more tolerant and are able to feel the need of the rest of humanity, they will accept what comes to them, knowing that they are helping the rest of their brethren to work out human karma. The understanding of this, dear brethren, will bring to you a true comprehension of brotherhood.

Brotherhood does not mean just doing as you like. Brotherhood means sharing, sharing both the blessings and the sufferings of your fellows; accepting with humility and faith the divine law which is at work on this earth plane—divine law working through the hearts of men and women, working through all human life, teaching lessons, revealing to all people the difference between good and evil, between selflessness and selfishness.

The wrongs in the world cannot be put right by legislation alone. They can only be put right through the human heart. And do remember that people are not all at the same level of evolution spiritually; and those who may have climbed a little higher up the mountain should not look critically on their brethren on the lower slopes. They should regard all men and women with love—not even with pity, but with love—knowing that all are moving up the mountain slopes until at last they reach the apex of the mountain when they become clothed in gold; not the gold of earth but that lovely gold of God—the gold of love.

This, my friends, is what we call the golden harvest. Every single soul will come to it. It matters not who you are, or what you are, you all have that spark of light within you. And if you do your best to follow that inner light, which means being loving and kind, humble and gentle in thought, in act—it is so simple—you grow all the time. But more than this, you are opening the main centre of your being, your heart, to receive the blessing of the Great White Light which is pouring down upon you as the sunlight pours down upon the seed.

Jesus once said that not a sparrow falls to the ground *without your Father; but the very hairs on your head are all numbered*. Now, if you could see a diagram of life as it can be seen in the Halls of Wisdom in the spirit world you would see a most intricate criss-cross pattern—innumerable little lines crossing and crossing again and again, backwards

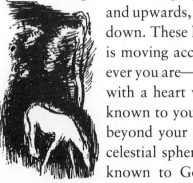

and upwards, forwards and across, up and down. These lines have a purpose, and all is moving according to divine law. Whoever you are—even you, my child, possibly with a heart which is breaking—you are known to your guide and to the brethren beyond your guide, the great ones in the celestial spheres; and most of all are you known to God, your heavenly Father–Mother, your Creator. All your need is known, whether it be physical or spiritual. And everything which happens to you has a purpose.

You must have seen for yourself how one thing leads to another. You all know how you are brought to meet the right people, to come to the right place at the right time. Because God knows your need His

24

messengers are sent to guide and help you. Every single detail of life is watched over and cared for. All people will come to understand in time that there is a divine Intelligence and Love which has humanity in its care, and however much men and women seem to suffer there is always a merciful power which comes to the aid of the suffering; and *you*, remember, may be a channel for God to help your fellow beings. You will sometimes feel moved to say certain words. Sometimes you say them and other times you shrink and say 'I don't like to'. But if you can always act and speak with love and tolerance you will, we assure you, be doing the work of the angels.

But mankind will not be forever imprisoned in a body of flesh. Remember the golden harvest which awaits every soul. Time is nothing, a thousand years is but a day; and all men and women are proceeding on the path upward to the golden world of God— where they will live in an indestructible and eternal body of light.

When you enter the spirit world at death, when you have freed yourself from the entanglements of the physical body, your eyes are opened, and you see the glory of the heavens irradiate with the light. In the spirit world you will find that everything you look upon will be illumined with an inner light and the colours will be beyond anything you can imagine with your earthly mind. But if you can just for a flash picture a scene of utmost beauty illumined with

25

heavenly light from within, so that it is radiating and pulsating colour and harmony and beauty, you will form some idea of what you will find in the world of spirit, providing that to the best of your ability you have taken light into yourself whilst living in a physical body. You do this by *giving* love, my brethren.

CHAPTER III

SPIRIT IS LIFE

We come with great joy to commune with you. The message that we have to convey is that of the eternal life to which the human soul may awaken. Some, we know, dread the very thought of living on beyond death; to others the idea would seem to mean an eternal clinging to this material world, to material conditions and to the possessions which they have accumulated. Such possessions need not be of a material nature; possessions of the mind become dear to some; some have a possessive attitude towards people they love. While it is easy to decry this, if we analyze for ourselves our own reactions to life, we may discover that we too are possessive, not only on this physical plane but also in the spiritual worlds.

What do we mean by 'eternal life'? We mean something transcending this mortal life, transcending even that life in the beyond to which the soul passes. We mean a breaking away from, a casting-off of mortality, and the emergence and triumph of the spirit over man's frailty and limitation. We mean, as Jesus said, that man must be born again out of his old mortal self: that the old Adam must die so that the new man may live. No words of ours can give you the true conception of what this emergence from the toils of mortality can unveil, nor of the peace, freedom and happiness of the soul centred on God. Rightly did Jesus speak of this state as the kingdom of heaven, for this it literally is. Nor is it available only to the soul freed from flesh. Even while in incarnation man can enter the presence of God, can abide in God, and know bliss. Many of the saints have done so. Any soul may follow the path which leads to the kingdom, and none is barred therefrom.

Let us examine two aspects of human life. The most dominant is that of the physical and the material life; but the second aspect lies buried deep in the subconsciousness until it is quickened and brought out into the conscious. We refer to the spiritual life—the life of the innermost. To many the material life has the greater claim to their attention. In a sense this is right, for it is through the physical life that the soul garners the experiences by which it grows towards God. But this is not the whole truth. Both aspects must be recognized, attuned and perfectly balanced, but the first and fundamental aspiration of man should be towards spirit. It is no use thinking that man's spiritual life can wait, for the progress and happiness of mankind depends on man's understanding of this attunement and balance between matter and spirit. Not until the human soul on this earth learns to recognize the spiritual life as the supreme light and purpose of its being will it find that great joy in the beyond which is its birthright.

Material and physical life must be based upon that eternal life of the spirit which is supreme, and which had its being yesterday, lives today, and will live forever. Eternal life is not something to look forward to in some future world of ease and joy. Eternal life is a divine knowledge and consciousness of God to which you can awaken at any moment, here and now. . . . *Ye know neither the day nor the hour wherein the Son of Man cometh.* What does this mean? It means that no soul can know how soon a consciousness of God's perpetual presence will break through into its being. And when that moment comes it will know the meaning of eternity; it will enter into the lifestream of eternal life, consciously.

Here then is your goal and your purpose; this is the end for which you have all been created—to enter consciously into this stream of God-life. When this happens you will know that you are in your brother's or sister's heart and he or she in yours—that you are together in God, that all life is in God, and that you cannot be separate from any part of it; that in God is eternal life and truth. God is the supreme power, the wisdom and the love in which all life is held.

We know, better perhaps than you think, just how

acute and difficult human suffering can be. We also know there is one sure comfort and healing to be found, one source of peace for every man, woman and child. Only by withdrawal of consciousness from the outer world to the inner reality will the soul find peace in the midst of war, safety in danger.

What does this mean? In very simple words it means surrender of the self; complete surrender of every problem, every discomfort, every difficulty with which you are surrounded. Yes, my brethren, even your troubles must be surrendered to God—which is perhaps the thing which most people are the most reluctant to do, for we are apt to cling to trouble. It is easy for us who dwell in spirit to say these things, we know; nevertheless it is simple truth we give you, that in this surrender to the Supreme, to the Great Spirit, lies the secret of happiness, of health, of love. This does not mean for a moment that you should neglect your service and your work in the world. The act of surrender takes place in your innermost self. It comes to the soul in moments of deep quiet, when the soul has withdrawn from outer turmoil, confusion and sorrow. Never cling to your sorrows. Let all these fall from you, and if you do go through a period of difficulty and trials and perhaps disillusion, remember the words: *Again, a little while, and ye shall see me*.

This is the voice of the Son of God speaking. That Son of God is not a separate entity dwelling far away in heaven, but the light of God which can shine through you and your brother and sister. Only for a space does he seem to depart; and then he will return . . . if you seek him. Try it, my brethren, when next you are possessed by fear, anger, anxiety, or perplexity. Be still; raise your thoughts to the Supreme. Surrender all problems, all troubles. Yield everything up to God; and the light will return and so illumine you that you will know your path; and at the end of that path waits the entry to the kingdom.

Whilst the soul is bound by physical possessions and desires it cannot see or know truth. Therefore it remains unconscious of its own nature; but when a soul is raised above all such limitations it knows that life is eternal. It begins to recognize feelings which are actual memories of its own past. The true home of your spirit, my brother and my sister, is not here, bound by matter, but in a realm of light and glory. At any moment of your life here on earth you can make contact with that realm, your spiritual home. Is it not good after a hard day's work to go home, where all is peaceful and restful? So it is with your labour here on earth; at any moment, when you have practised the art of true communion with your higher self and your spirit, you can enter in, if only for a flash, to your spiritual home.

In spirit there is no time; all is the eternal present—and a flash can last a thousand years in the spirit life. Those of you who mourn some loved one may feel that our words are poor comfort. You will ask: 'Where is my own dear one? What you tell me gives me the idea that my loved one has gone to some distant heaven that I can't reach.' Again your heart feels its loneliness and desires to possess the presence of the beloved. We assure you that nothing can separate you from one you love. You are with him, with her, in your innermost being, for the spirit world *is* the inner plane, the world of spirit is an inner world, yet it is all about you. We do not live alone, my brethren. Mingling with us, all around, are the radiant souls of those who have entered into the land of light. They come close. Were it not for the help of such spiritual beings the human spirit would recede ever deeper into matter; but because God wants His children to become alive and quickened to the spiritual worlds around He sends messengers, angel beings, teachers and saviours to humanity.

All through the ages the secret ones have laboured amongst humankind to help them to understanding, to a quickening of their innermost. This is the reason for the communion of spirit, the communion of saints, not that the man or woman should draw spirit down into that condition of life from which it has been released, but that all may be raised up. The meaning is plain—that all who have knowledge of spiritual life and communion with the higher worlds should raise their aspiration and their consciousness to the place of complete surrender to divine love. This life of spiritual aspiration and meditation will not incapacitate you for your duty in the material world. If you have surrendered all to God and recognized that of your earthly self you are nothing and can do nothing, if you have recognized that it is the spirit of God working through you that accomplishes the work, then you will be doing God's work and you cannot fail.

Keep this love of the spirit alive in your heart. Let it be your guiding light. All is love. God is love. Life is love.

CHAPTER IV

GOD IS MOTHER AS WELL AS FATHER

Once spirit comes to dwell in matter it starts to create what is called soul. Soul is the creation of feeling; it is that part of your being built up because of the experiences of earth life, through which the tender inner self is touched. It is through man's feelings, either of pain or joy, that his soul is created. The soul of the world is the *feeling* of the world. The soul of a nation is created by the life of feeling of the people of that nation. The life of the nation creates the soul of the nation. Soul can also be described as the feminine aspect of life, the Mother principle which exists in everyone. It is the tenderness, the love, the gentleness in life without which spiritual death must ensue.

The first principle of life is the divine Will, the Father or masculine aspect, and from the first principle was created the Mother or woman aspect, that which gives form to creation. The old story in Genesis says that the woman (or soul) was taken from the rib, or the region of the heart, of the first creation, Adam, while Adam was asleep or quiescent. In other words, from the first principle, the male, the second principle of life, the female, or woman, was brought forth.

Lacking a soul, the first principle could not continue to live, could not evolve. Adam needed that second aspect. He had to become *ensouled* to live, for the soul gives feeling to the human self.

In the coming age will come a development of intuition and an increase of soul power among the people of the earth. The Father or the Will aspect will be balanced by the Mother or the Intuition aspect. When there is a perfect blending of these two principles of creation, then the Christ child is brought forth.

Do not mistake our meaning: all people contain both qualities within themselves—both the manly and the womanly qualities. Each individual passes through many trials, tribulations, initiations, by which process the two principles of Will and Love gradually become united and perfectly balanced. Thus we may see the Christ manifesting in perfectly-evolved souls whom the world hails as avatars or saviours.

We would therefore speak to you more about the transforming power which is within all children of God, the divine light which can transform your earthliness and make you truly sons and daughters of God. We often speak to you about the Christ light within your hearts. You will grow weary maybe of the repetition of this one truth; but it is the only truth in life. It is therefore vitally important that you comprehend more and more of the light of God in yourselves, and above all as it manifests in His supreme Son, Christ, Lord of the earth planet. How can you best realize more of this light within yourselves in your daily life? Quite simply, by putting into effect the words of Jesus—*love one another*. Those three words, if truly understood and lived, would set the whole world aflame with power, with happiness and with plenty.

We would add that this love must extend to all God's creatures, for how can the human family expect anything but a reaction of pain and suffering for itself when it is cruel to brother animal? Cruelty is a terrible sin, my children, cruelty in action, thought and speech. Tame animals have to depend upon men and women. They give them their faith; they look to them for food, protection and companionship; but pain is sometimes inflicted upon them thoughtlessly, selfishly and carelessly. The blessing of peace and true brotherhood will only come to you as you learn to treat all God's creatures—yes, and the very earth itself—kindly, with imagination, and with respect. As we have said before, 'respect all life, for all is of God'.

What happens when the soul simply and wholly lives to love and serve its fellow creatures? That soul is strengthening the link between its spirit and the Great Spirit, all-glorious, all-powerful, almighty, the blazing Sun of light. By power of love, contact between the soul and God is confirmed, and light pours into the soul. Then it is building the body of light which is the wedding garment spoken of in Jesus's parable. No soul, even though it passes from the physical, can enter into the heavenly life unless it is thus clothed in light.

Through all religions you will find instruction in how to bring into operation this light of the spirit which lies dormant in every human being. The whole purpose of life in the flesh is to develop this power, through love—not through any mental pursuit, which is the mistake many are making in this mental age of Aquarius. Many people read book after book after book, and their brains are filled with reading matter. But something more is needed—the wisdom of the heart, and love; because love is the light. Your mental body may be very strong; but unless your heart is filled with love and the desire to give loving service you cannot use the knowledge which you have acquired. You cannot even control it; it will control you. It will absorb you. This is why the development of the simple light of love in the heart is so important at the present time, because without it the immense power of this mental age is likely to destroy and absorb people. Don't be fearful about this, for we are telling you of the counteracting influence. We only emphasize the danger of this mental stimulation without a corresponding goodness of heart and loveliness of character.

Within you all lies opportunity to grow in spirit, to grow in stature until you become as the Master. Hold the ideal ever before you. Be strong in spirit, do not be cast down. It is good to recognize shortcomings, for humility is a true companion of the aspirant on the path; keep your feet on the earth, yes: but lift your face towards the heavens, for the light which floods into you from on high will steady your feet and guide them in the right path. Have confidence in this divine light. Surrender to it with a tranquil mind and a heart full of love for God. We are not speaking of some nebulous and incomprehensible force, far distant from you. This divine fire is within your very being, and as you raise your face and open your heart to the Sun, the rays of the Sun stimulate the divine light within you. Work to bring this light into manifestation in you, not in haste, but quietly, gently, with mind and heart fixed steadily upon God.

Seek and ye shall find. The Master did not speak idly. The soul which seeks always finds. Sometimes the answer is found instantly; sometimes a whole life may be lived before the answer comes, but come it will, for there is always an answer to the search of the soul.

We know that it is not easy to extricate yourselves when you are immersed in the concerns of the material plane. We too have our limitations; for we too are bound to some extent, as you are, by the nature of our service and work. We were once asked why we came back into the heaviness of the earth conditions, having gained our freedom. We said in answer, 'Because we love our companions on earth; we are attracted to their need, and know we must come back to help them.' Thus we all have to suffer a degree of bondage; but because there is love in the heart, it sweetens all our work. This also applies to you; when you feel love in your heart, you are calm and at peace and all rebellion leaves you.

We have often told you that love is the first requisite. Your scriptures say that you may have many gifts, but if you lack love you are 'as sounding brass or a tinkling cymbal'. Love is the key. When you feel love towards life, love towards the beauty of the earth and all God's creation, you are filled with joy and even ecstasy, and the smallest thing can bring you the deepest happiness. Moreover, as soon as you love, you long to give. It is perhaps an unconscious desire, but always when you love, you give.

We were talking to a friend a little while ago, someone for whom we have a deep and tender love. She was in great sorrow and longed for a reunion with a loved one who had passed on. But she felt so angry and even resentful about certain circumstances in her life that she created a barrier between herself and her happiness. Heaven was waiting for her, even though she was still living in a physical body, but she could not approach its gate because of her resentment.

Many things bar people from heaven, but anger and resentment above all. You have to make an effort to get over these obstacles, and pray to God with all your heart to help you to disperse those negative qualities which chain you to earth.

Can men and women ever understand that God intends them to be happy? That God does not punish them but rather that they inflict their own punishment on themselves? You bring forward arguments galore in order to deny this simple eternal truth; you cannot bear to be told that you are your own enemy, and that you bring your troubles to yourselves. Yet when, through constant outgiving of love, you have learnt to go into the heart of God, into the Christ heart, trouble has no longer any power over you. Only when you become bound down to earth are you immersed in trouble.

We are not advising you to try to rise into realms of glory to the neglect of your duties on earth. But if you reach a state of spiritual receptivity you will see everything in the correct perspective, and understand true values. You will understand that all the things that trouble you really matter very little. All you have to do is to deal day by day with little difficulties as they arise, remembering that there is a wisdom ever watching over you, bringing about harmony and making crooked places straight for you.

Many people do not admit the reality of divine

intelligence; they think that man has to battle for himself. Certainly you have to do *your* part, to work and to strive upwards, but also you have to recognize, humbly, that underneath are the everlasting arms, and that your Creator is merciful and loving. Those who have this realization find happiness and peace in spite of all difficulties. Their faith carries them forward.

This brings us to the question, 'How can we best help humanity to overcome its fear of war, and destruction'?* A great mountain of fear seems to be building up, and because of this, people think out more and more terrible weapons by which to protect themselves. These thoughts of fear build up an invisible foe far worse than the one you can see.

Yet there is really nothing for the human spirit to fear. While they concentrate only upon physical things, upon resulting pain and suffering, people feel tortured because they can do nothing; their hearts are wrung and they lose poise and faith. But if you are really reaching out towards God, if you are living with love in your heart, nothing can touch you.

You must realize that imagination plays a very important part in life; it is a gift which must be striven

*When this teaching was given, humanity was particularly gripped by the threat of nuclear war. We believe the words are still applicable, but to any of the collective fears that grip humanity, including that of ecological disaster, perhaps more in the forefront of people's minds today. A small editorial alteration has been made later to allow for this.

for and cultivated, but at the same time imagination of the negative kind can inflict unnecessary suffering. A constructive, positive imagination can be man's friend and helper, a negative imagination his foe. We would not make you disregardful of suffering, but we would like to say that the human body is so wonderfully constructed and the power of love is so great that there is a mercy which dims even the worst pain; and that love can and does work miracles. God is merciful as well as just, and as you probe the meaning of suffering you will recognize a merciful and loving power which succours and saves.

In the Apocryphal gospels, St John wrote that Jesus came to him even while his crucified body was apparently in agony on the cross. Yet Jesus the Christ was not suffering that agony, he was absent from his body. His spirit was with his disciples. Did he not say to them once, *The prince of this world cometh, and hath nothing in me?*

When the spirit rises above the body, the soul does not suffer. Do not allow this to make you indifferent to pain, for anyone who suffers needs all your love and your care; but we point out to you that man's spirit can rise above suffering, as Jesus demonstrated.

So we come back to humanity's fear of annihilation, whether through nuclear war or ecological disaster, and again we beg you to remember that there is a loving, protective power. There is a plan for mankind outside which it cannot stray; the child of

God has to learn to trust that power. God the Mother knows Her child and can apply an antidote to suffering, even as a human mother has an antidote to her child's suffering, and wisdom in guiding its tottering steps.

In the dawn of life souls were taught by the angelic messengers and by the light within them to worship the mother element. The great Mother was the adored one; but times changed and the worship of the Mother was forgotten.

Now times are changing yet again; and more and more, in days to come, will humanity come to recognize and to worship the Mother aspect of God, divine Mother, and to realize the nature of Her blessing and Her influence. More and more will leadership of and service to the world by women be realized, and through this the true balance of life will be restored. This perfect partnership, this true brotherhood/sisterhood of the spirit, is coming. But it must start with the individual. As the individual man and woman expand in spiritual consciousness, so the whole community will become harmonized.

With the coming of spiritual enlightenment there must be a strong stand against the attack, not of a physical enemy, but of ignorance; for ignorance brings fear. And liberation from fear will come through man's centering upon the light of the great

Sun, the Christ-spirit, Son of the Father–Mother God. As men and women learn how to open their consciousness to that spiritual light and life, all fear will depart, and they will grow in love and in confidence in each other.

We direct your vision towards the divine Mother, in perfect human form. We ask you to visualize Her presence in the form of a beautiful mother, the mother of heaven and earth. When the people of earth can return to worship of the beautiful Mother, source of all life, there will be a return to happiness. For the Christ which shines forth from your heart, and reveals all mysteries to you, is the child of the great Mother, and is born of love.

CHAPTER V

———

REMEMBRANCE

Have you ever thought what human life would be like if you all had no power to remember? In losing your power to remember, would you not feel robbed of one of the most wonderful gifts the Creator has given you?

Some of you may have memories of a kind which are too sad to recall. Yet memories hold the sweetest happiness even if they themselves are sad, because joy and sorrow are like inseparable twins; even in the depths of sorrow the human soul can find compensation which can only be described as joyful. There is always an uplifting element of beauty in sadness, always an element of sadness in joy. Therefore we can see how both aspects can arise together in memory, bringing beauty and solace to the soul.

We would take you into our particular land of memory, what we refer to as the infinite and eternal garden of the spirit. If you sit in meditation and contemplation you will find that your thoughts will come more easily if, in imagination, you can enter a peaceful garden, or the quiet countryside. Here you can feel very close to the heart of God. Now in past ages, in the beginning of life, beings from afar came to the earth to teach young humanity how to live happily there. This youthful company of human beings was first taught in that garden of the spirit— shall we call it the Garden of Eden? They were taught the laws of living both physical and spiritual. They learnt how to live healthily and happily on the physical plane and they were also taught the mysteries of heaven and of the companionship of angels.

A part of these mysteries was realization of the power and the help which the soul could receive during daily life by understanding how to live in harmony with the laws of nature. Souls were taught to reverence the divine spirit, the heavenly Father, and the Mother, the creative power which brought form into being. The Mother was most deeply venerated by the simple people of the past, because in the Mother they saw the symbol of birth and eternal life. Life came from the divine Mother, who created the form, used by divine spirit, the heavenly Father. Not only human form, but all form on this earth planet was created and given birth to by divine Mother. Thus the ancients worshipped God as Mother, as well as Father.

They were taught something more. They were taught that every creature born in matter embodied a part of those two, part of the Father, part of the Mother God. Therefore they understood that all life must be revered, all united in one grand family; and that all creation existed within a divine and illimitable circle.

You are told that in the beginning was the Word; and that Word was a vibration, a mighty sound which reverberated in ever-expanding circles. We suggest therefore that you think of your life as being held in a circle of light in which you are all enfolded; that all of you are living within that Word, within the circle of light and power and protection. All life is as one. All are brothers, sisters.

From this simple truth came the first religion ever known to humanity; it was a religion of brotherhood, of the brotherhood of the human spirit. The basis of all natural and spiritual life is brotherhood; this is cosmic law. To teach and demonstrate the meaning of brotherhood, groups or brotherhoods were formed and have existed in all parts of the world since the beginning. In the spirit world too you will discover how faithfully people in the spirit meet in their temples and lodges, and how they worship and serve as members of a vast brotherhood.

All this seems a long way from our original words about remembrance; but when you look back over your life, remembering what you as an individual have received as a result of service, sacrifice and love of others, some of whom existed before you were ever born, you can only do so with wonder and gratitude. Let us therefore remember all the service we and you have received from the great brotherhood of life, from all the saints and sages who have lived to serve God and humanity. For had it not been for the lives of these sainted ones, life as known today on this earth would no longer exist. You all owe your very existence, and everything you enjoy today, to the servers of the past, those who lived to serve God first, and then to serve their country, and then to serve their friends and comrades. This is a truth, my friends, which is vitally important for every man or woman to understand; no-one can live to themselves, since everyone is dependent on their comrades, on their brothers and sisters. Therefore we remember with love and thankfulness all men and women who have given their lives in service to humankind.

*

Try to regard the physical body only as the clothing of the soul, the outer coat. When you have reached to the centre, to the truth which is God, spirit, you will only be conscious of eternally living and will not be separated at any time from those you love and have loved. In that state of cosmic consciousness you are united with all you love, for in love there is no separation. If you who are listening to these words have lost dear companions by the release of the spirit, if you have lost the physical form, we advise you to use your thought-power and create in your minds, *see* your loved ones. Think of them, speak to them spirit to spirit. This takes a little time for you to understand, but if you persevere in your quiet moments in

48

thinking of the spirit world as always there, always being brought into vision and manifestation, you will eventually live in that consciousness of life, not in all its drabness and suffering and restriction as in a physical body, but a life in which the spirit is free as the lark in the sky.

Each one of you has your own particular fear, and what you on earth would call a little trouble. No-one on earth is completely without some problem; it may seem only a small problem to others, but a very big one to you. Now we want you to consider this question of fear and loneliness and the problems which affect you in your daily life, sometimes very deeply. We want you to understand that we of the Brotherhood of the Great White Light who dwell in the world of spirit and the celestial world are not without knowledge of your particular difficulty. We love you and want to help you. Many of you were companions of ours in former lives and we feel the relationship between ourselves and you. You think only of your present incarnation, and many of you may think that you live through three score years and ten and then you are finished. Oh no, you are far from finished—you have only just begun! Life is not just for three score years and ten, but for eternity, and is continually unfolding.

A wonderful provision has been made for you and every human being by the wise and loving Father–Mother God, and this provision is that there are periods in your life when you leave your hard work on earth and withdraw from the physical into a heavenly state, and there in that world of beauty and harmony you are refreshed and strengthened. You on earth cannot conceive of the beauty which awaits you in what your orthodox friends call heaven. You know how you all feel after you have had a lovely holiday—you return to work feeling full of energy and strength and ready to continue your very interesting work. This is the point: your *interesting* work.

Some of you feel that your work is far from interesting, that it is wearying and boring, but you alone can make your life's work interesting, and will do so if you are seeking for the blessing of all life. Whatever your chosen task or whatever work God has placed before you we say—accept it with thankfulness. Do your best and God will do the rest. It is for you to make the best of whatever conditions you are in. Make the best of life, be thankful for life itself, and keep your vision on a goal, which is all good.

Now you all come to a point at some time or another in your life when you have an ordeal before you and you are afraid. Fear is man's greatest enemy. You fear your ordeal, you fear perhaps an operation or a big change in your life, you fear changing conditions because you know that you are entering the unknown. Most people fear death, because they do not know the meaning of death. We in spirit have passed through death many times—and so have you, but your memory is blocked because you are in the valley. If you had risen to the heights you would have a clearer vision and you would know that there is no death, only a change of conditions, only a different state of life. There is nothing to fear in death, for you do not die.

If you look back over your life you will know that what you most feared never happened. You found yourself facing an ordeal which you could not avoid, but when it came to the point there was a most heavenly power which carried you unscathed through the experience you dreaded.

We want you to think about this because it will help you to make your contact in full consciousness with the Great Spirit, with that all-enfolding love which teaches you that all is well for him who loves God. A child has to trust its parent, and the parent must be worthy of that trust. Man's own experience teaches him to trust his divine parents, because again and again it is proved to him that God is all wise, God *is* love, and that what comes to man in life comes to him because of the divine law which is love. When you break the law of love you are unhappy, you are distraught, you are fearful. You fight to escape the dilemma, not realizing that there is this law of love which, when man obeys it, when he or she applies it to daily life all problems dissolve. There are no problems, only God is there. Most people fear change, and when change comes, they wonder what

51

is going to happen to them. Instead they could feel, 'God is wise, I place my hand in the hand of God, knowing that all change is for my good.' When all people know this then the world will reflect the kingdom of heaven.

We are going to suggest to you our brethren that the vision on which you keep your gaze should be the six-pointed star, the symbol of the spirit, symbol of the spirit of Christ. As you hold your vision steadily and firmly on that star you will find yourself being drawn up so that you see things on your earth from a higher vantage point. When you view things from the valley, you cannot see the beauty which surrounds you in clear perspective, but when you are drawn up by the star to a higher level, you see the various conditions and problems of life quite differently. All humanity needs to follow the star. It will never lead you astray, never misguide you.

Always remember to apply divine law to your problems. If you do this, you can never go wrong.

And so to old and young we say, keep on keeping on, with squared shoulders and head high. Keep right on to that world of light where there will be a great welcome for you in a beautiful home, in which you may rest for a while to gain refreshment before going forth once again to serve and to love and be loved.

CHAPTER VI

CREATING BEAUTIFUL LIFE

Man is part of God, and God is a creator. The precious gift which God has given to His child on earth is the power to create. A human being does not need an abundance of material wealth to create beauty and harmony. These come primarily from within his heart. There is beauty in simplicity, harmony in his environment only because he himself is harmonious.

Now this is exactly what happens in the spirit world. Out of man's soul emanations conditions are created in which the individual soul lives a better, a finer but a very similar life to that formerly lived on earth. The whole point is that man comes down to live in a physical body with opportunities of developing within himself the Christ-being. Did not Jesus say to his followers that 'What I do, you can do also'? He came to demonstrate the real way to truth and life. What a wonderful gift God has given to all His children in this power to create, the power within to expand, to grow, and the power to help their fellow creatures! But if man does not make use of that power in order to serve his fellow creatures he is wasting his opportunities. This is the power of life, the power which heals.

True beauty is created by pure thought, lovely thought, lovely imagination. Thus are you now at this very moment creating your etheric, your soul world, the world in which you will live when you have passed away from the physical body. You are creating also the world in which you live now.

Some of you are puzzled about what is called 'imagination', particularly when you are thinking of heavenly things and the spiritual world. You wonder if what you see in your meditation and in your contemplation of beauty is real, or is it merely the result of imagination? We would emphasize to you, anything which you strongly imagine, you begin to create in soul substance. When you create in your mind or in your imagination you are creating *actual* form in the soul world. Imagination is the doorway, the key into the soul world. What you imagine to be there *is* there, and enduring. So you will see that by your thought, by your imagination, you have the power to create real form in the soul world, and that form can become externalized in the physical world.

True happiness originates from the soul and from the spirit, and in order to attain happiness the person must reach upward and aspire to heavenly conditions. Nevertheless the majority of men and women live blind and deaf to the spiritual worlds and cut off from their higher self, their real self which lives and has its being in God.

If you could see your whole self you would be overwhelmed with astonishment. When you look at yourself in a mirror you see a physical body possessing certain characteristics, and you think that body is you. But if you could see with the vision of your soul, or through the eyes of your celestial body, you would see that you comprise not only a physical body, but a form which, seen from the spirit planes of life, appears as a star of great light and radiance. At the base of this radiant star you would see a small, dark triangle which is your physical body, your physical being, but above and around the physical body is this radiant light. You will ask, 'does this apply to *every* man and woman, even those who are cruel and wicked?' Yes, it applies to every man and woman, for all are sons or daughters of God, and all contain within themselves the same potentialities. Every soul born of God has the opportunity to aspire and rise to the apex of the star which surrounds him and become part of the star.

Now in this star—which is a form living in the etheric and yet reaching to the heavenly worlds—are degrees or planes of consciousness or understanding. In this star are all the planes of life concentrated upon one central, focal point, man—man's mind, his soul, and even his body—and within man lies the power to reach out to those realms of spiritual life and wisdom and knowledge. Immediately beyond or within the physical life is what is known as the etheric or the soul world; this world is composed of people's thoughts and aspirations and hopes, where their inmost thoughts and desires become manifest. You are told that the next world is real and solid to those who inhabit it. Indeed, it is more real than your physical world, because it is more enduring, being made of a substance which is nearer the eternal than physical substance. This etheric world is the world of the soul, the world to which you will pass when you leave your physical body. It is the world from which we have all come. And even whilst in a physical body you may draw from this world soul substance which clothes your spirit and finds manifestation in physical matter. We mean that as you aspire, as you seek to live in constant awareness of the real life of the spirit, so you will be able to recreate your physical life, for within your own heart lies the creative power of God, the power to recreate and perfect your own life, and that of the world around you.

The soul which reaches its state of bliss is not wholly perfect, is still the rough ashlar, needing the training ground of a physical world's experiences. In time it will feel within itself that it must be more active in God's service. So that soul comes back again to earth to carry on a work, the nature of which it has been shown from above. It sees the great need for its help, its service, and willingly comes back. Only when the soul awakens to this glorious vision of service does it come; it is not forced back. The desire must come to the soul's innermost being. This is the way God's laws work—slowly, quietly. God does not force, but guides and inspires. As the flower grows from the bulb so does man grow and develop until at last he passes through his final degree, the highest degree. Then shall the temple bells ring out: 'This man is the Christ man.' That is *your* future, the future of every one of you here.

Look down the ages and you will see the Christed ones stand forth again and again and again. You are asking, 'What about all the millions of souls—will they all become Christed?' Yes, because the seed-atom of the Christ is within each one.

Look out upon a clear starlit night and see the countless stars above. Each one of those is Christed, is a Christ, a creator, a teacher, a saviour working, creating, evolving life. It is not possible for man's physical brain to comprehend anything beyond its physical limitations, so be content to know that all life is governed by divine law, that you are all cared for and loved, that there is no death. Yes, the soul outlives its clothing, enters into greater opportunity and joy, and in spirit there is no separation. You cannot be separated from love.

CHAPTER VII

HEARING THE VOICE WITHIN

To find truth you must experience it in your soul. You can read hundreds of books, or study the religions of all time, and find that all of them have one common point, one common denominator: and this is *love*—which is another word for light or soul illumination. To realize this soul illumination you have to shut away the clamour of the lower mind, to become humble, very simple. Shall we try to explain it more clearly? Then imagine that you come into a temple to worship God. Now God is *in* you but God is also *outside* you. God is speaking to you both through nature and through your fellow beings, and in your inmost spirit. Through every experience, everything that happens in your life, God is speaking to you. God is your teacher, so think of God as being in your heart. God is actually *here*, within your heart. In other words, the higher aspect of you is God.

Of course all life comes forth from God; darkness and light are both alike to God; the whole of creation is of God. We do want you to understand that you yourself are also a part of God, that God is speaking in you, so whenever you enter a temple of worship, even this small sanctuary, in your imagination, you can kneel before an altar of light, and in silence wait for God to speak.

How will God speak to you? In a 'feeling' which will come to you, a feeling of worship. As you kneel before that altar you worship, you thank God . . . for life, for your friends, for your happiness, for sunshine and rain, for flowers and birds and animals, and for all the wonderful inventions making life easier and happier. Oh, the wealth of gifts that you could thank God for! Not least of your thankfulness should be for the companionship of your fellow creatures, for all those who have been instruments of God to bless your life. If you will only think back you will find there are great numbers of people whom you should thank. So, as you kneel before that altar, you will be pouring out blessing—for thankfulness is blessing. To feel truly thankful brings the outpouring of blessing upon life, even blessing upon God.

To be sure that what you learn from listening to our talks is true you must ask yourself, do you feel instinctively that it is truth? Yes, your spirit does feel thus impressed; but your earthly mind, mostly concerned with the activities of physical life, questions your spirit. As all wise people will tell you, that mind can be the slayer of truth. When that mind starts to analyze in a critical way, it is demolishing truths which by itself it can never restore. The mind

59

demolishes; but the spirit of truth that is within will never lie, will never mislead you—*never*.

Therefore whenever you feel that you want guidance, put aside all thoughts of self, or what *you* think you want. Don't allow your own desires to interfere with that pure light of God which can flow direct into your heart. What your heart tells you is truth is true indeed. To arrive at truth you must become very humble, very simple in yourself. The great people are those who are simple in heart. '"I come in simple ways, in lowly ways," saith the Lord.'

Now, my children, life is ruled by law, and whatever you do brings a result. Even what you think

sows a seed in you which grows. If it is not a good thought it will depress you; if it is a good thought, a hopeful thought, a God-thought, it will expand and bring you joy. The brethren in the world of spirit are exceedingly happy because they are peaceful in their hearts, undisturbed by dark happenings. You will say, 'Is it right to be undisturbed by the dark things?' And we reply, 'Yes, my child, because by maintaining inner peace and letting the light burn steadily within you, you are doing far more good to your fellow creatures and to the world than if you get excited and argumentative with other people about disagreeable conditions.' Keep your poise. Be steady on your path. Perhaps you have to face some unpleasant moments with problems which you do not quite know how to deal with; you may get unhappy or excited about these things. Now can you remember all your lives what White Eagle says now? 'Be still. Keep very still and quiet within. Ask, and God or your guardian angel will help you.' Maybe you won't understand that you are being helped by someone *outside* yourself, but it will work. So, be still inside. Keep very calm and let the power of God assist you as it will.*

We are very earnest in this, and to all our brothers and sisters we give the same message. Some of you have to face sickness and presently old age; some have to face frustration, or endure very hard work, or suffer disappointment; most of you feel that you are carrying a heavy burden. Are you meant to throw your burdens away and become care-less? No, but you have to recognize the value of all these things, and to see beyond them. Pray to see what these burdens can teach you. Sometimes the question arises, 'What am I to do? Am I to do this or that? Do I stay, go here or go there?' Our answer to such questions is this: do the job which God has placed immediately before you. Have you ever thought that your work has been placed before you by God in order to give you an opportunity to develop your character, your spiritual sensitivity and gifts, and also as an opportunity to help others also by your example? We wonder

*As some of the expressions in this paragraph indicate, this is the talk to young people referred to in the Preface.

61

sometimes how many of our brethren remember this point—the example that they are setting in the world?

Before you all opens a path of light which is leading you onward and upward to someday attain to indescribable happiness and satisfaction because you will have fulfilled the real purpose of life. When man fulfils this purpose he is filled with peace and happiness. We know, we know, about your present-day sorrows and the problems that you must face. We know how you feel. We too can feel exactly the same because we feel *through you*, we feel *with you*; but always we know that this heavenly power is working, working, working through all the affairs of the individual, slowly to bring about illumination of their soul and their eventual happiness.

Never look back with regret; that is a waste of time. Do your best honourably. Let that inner voice speak, whatever the circumstances in which you are placed. Be careful what you say. Guard the 'unruly member' because the tongue can hurt others and it can make much mischief. So be careful what you say. Always speak the truth. Does this sound rather like a Sunday School talk? No. We are really going deeply into truth.

CHAPTER VIII

MASTER OF MATTER

Truth is within you. It takes no rise from outer things. Whatever your mind may believe, there is an inner-most centre in you all where truth abides in fullness. If you allow that inner light to guide you away from foolishness and belief in wrong values, then you will indeed be responding to truth; and having found truth, remember to have faith in that truth to guide you every step of your journey through life.

Are you tired of White Eagle bidding you, 'Keep on keeping on'? Believe us, it is the only way; because if you do not, you waste time running around corners, and presently find yourself in a cul-de-sac. Keep quietly on, and remember that you have been given a particular piece of work, because *you* are the only one who can do that work.

When you are doing your work, *do it easily*. Do your best, but happily and quietly and let it be a joy, not a burden. Relax, *in your mind*. Be happy, feel loving, and all things will work together for good. If God wants you to make a change He will make it for you. If there is no indication and nothing new is thrust before you, you can quite happily keep on quietly getting joy out of life. God has His own way of paying debts, God has His own way of helping His sons and daughters, even with material gifts.

We hope that you are coming to realize what a wonderful blessing has been offered to you in this knowledge of a spirit life and of a world much more beautiful than earth.

Many people will ask why they should bother about a world they cannot see. 'Let heaven take care of itself,' they say. But do you not see, dear ones, that *everything* depends on how man's life on the physical plane is spent; because only there can he develop the finer qualities of spiritual life, which give him power whilst still in the body to overcome death?

One of the most striking realizations of the soul when it momentarily escapes from earth's bondage during meditation, or perhaps receives a flash of cosmic consciousness, is that there is no death. Many people, particularly the Spiritualists, are likewise convinced that there is no death, because they have received messages and 'proof' from loved ones who have died. But such happenings represent only an infinitesimal part of this truth.

We remind you again of Jesus's words: *He that believeth on me, the works that I do shall he do also.* Now, what were these works? He possessed a miraculous power of healing; he could also raise the dead to life. He could give the most profound and beautiful truths to humanity in his parables. At the end he refused to save himself from crucifixion although he had power to do so, because he still had a work to do. That work was to demonstrate to humanity that man cannot be killed, even by crucifixion, even by murder. Jesus demonstrated this, and more. Most of you here in this congregation could stand up to testify that you too have received communications from spirits who have passed on. But you have yet to see the arisen body of the communicator. Yet Jesus said: *the works that I do shall he do also*. What does this mean? We will tell you.

In every man and woman dwell latent powers which when developed can enable them to leave their body at will and, while retaining full consciousness, travel to higher spheres. This procedure becomes normal and natural to one whom you may call a master, or to a disciple of a master. When the physical body has served its purpose, the master can lay it down and go on into another world—one that he is already accustomed to visiting. A master can at all times move freely in the spirit world. He does not know death. Death does not exist for him. But Jesus went a step beyond this, journeying to and fro between worlds. He was able so to change the atoms of his body by spiritual power, or the power of God, that his very body became transmuted, translated from dense flesh to a more etherealized or spiritualized state. Do you not remember his words: *Touch me not for I am not yet ascended to my Father*?

Other advanced souls, not only of this earth but on other planets who have achieved a similar degree of mastership, are able, as Jesus was, to change the actual physical atom.

We do not want to take you too deeply into these matters. Keep your feet on the earth, brethren, because you have to live on it. But don't allow it to become the one and only form of life in which to live.

Some people think that Jesus is alone the Son of God, not understanding that every human soul that is born is equally a son–daughter, in that man is created in God's own image and has been endowed with Godlike qualities. So when these qualities become quickened, are brought to life and unfolded, you eventually become master—master first of all of yourself, having control over your emotions, over your thoughts, over your body, and then over your conditions or environment. In other words, every human being becomes master of matter, and master of life itself. Many of you think that this attainment lies so far away that it is hardly worth the attempt.

Don't be so easily discouraged! Remember that the tiniest seed, which is hardly visible, can produce the most beautiful and perfect flower. Let us take for an illustration a lily with its roots deep in the damp earth. Emerging silently from darkness, it grows until the leaves and then the bud appears. Then at last, when the sun shines upon it, the lily opens its petals. And oh, how beautiful, how perfect is that flower!

You see, there is something altogether beautiful waiting for you. You will not always be bound down to a life with many perplexities and much suffering. No indeed; when you can once enter into the consciousness of God-life, you will break away from all such limitations. This is what the beloved Master Jesus came to demonstrate.

Can you at your present stage of development even begin to find these wonderful things about which we tell? Yes, you can start immediately; he or she who would tread the probationary path which leads to God must begin very simply. Jesus told us all how to live—*love one another*. Oh yes, at this we can register your thoughts. You are thinking, 'How can we ever learn to love so-and-so?' or, 'How can we ever love people who seem so naturally antagonistic to us, or people who commit terrible crimes?' But peace, my children ... peace ... be still; be at peace first of all in your own hearts, for this is the one way ever to establish peace, goodwill and brotherhood on your earth. Be patient; these things are coming. First of all, just examine your daily habits of thought, especially any antagonistic or critical thoughts, and even spoken criticism which can destroy the beautiful lily which has just started to grow in your heart—or in your brother's or sister's heart. The one who would become a disciple must start *on himself*, with love in the heart. The first and most important act is for the soul to refrain from intolerance—and from believing the worst. You cannot do any harm by reversing the process—by believing in the best in a person and encouraging that best to come forth.

Learn to live in an upright and honourable way yourself, 'doing unto others as you would be done unto'. Before all things love God, your Creator, and give thanks for your creation. Give thanks for the little light which is already burning within your soul and in the souls of your companions. Be thankful and keep on keeping on. Persevere, persevere, persevere on the spiritual path. Endeavour always to open your eyes to the reality of the unseen life, which is far, far more important than the material life which dominates humankind. Look beyond, beyond, my children, to that state of life which is perfect—perfectly beautiful—perfect in every detail! *Eye hath not seen, nor ear heard . . . the things which God hath prepared for them that love him.*

Instead of fearing death, substitute something better. Develop the power to go for a walk in higher realms! See for yourself their glory. No, we are not talking nonsense. The person who says there is nothing but physical matter is the one who is merely talking nonsense; not the one who describes the invisible worlds.

We leave you with this thought: do your best to uphold the truth of the invisible life and of the power which flows from that life to assist humanity. Be true to the light in your soul, which leads humanity from the unreal to the real country, to the eternal life.

CHAPTER IX

THE ROAD TO JOY

You are living today in an age of the mind, when humanity is worshipping the power of the mind. You do not realize that when you worship the mind, you are worshipping something which can destroy you body and soul, can destroy the very planet. You see, children of earth, all truth comes from spirit, but not everything which comes into the mind comes from spirit. Only when humanity recognizes that within the heart chakra lies the shining jewel of truth, and will submit to the guidance of the spirit within, will it find truth and happiness. The guidance within, which you call in-tuition, tuition from within, can then unfold beautifully and reveal to you your God-given, Godlike powers.

You know, my children, the enlightened ones of all time have found this truth. They have found the inner secret, this beautiful shining jewel within the lotus of the heart chakra, this shining jewel of truth. We heard a younger brother say: 'But we have a mind, White Eagle, and our mind demands to know the reason why.' 'Why ... why ... why?' is the eternal question of that material mind! My son, my daughter, you have a right to know and you will know—when you look in the right way and in the right direction for the answer to your question.

It is the desire to cling to your own personal self which limits, which holds you back. Realize that towards God only must you reach—that you of yourself are nothing—and forget the self and seek only to attain to that mystery we call God. Once break down the limitations of self and you will realize, you will know . . . truth. And even then you lose nothing worthwhile by losing yourself, but rather, knowing yourself and knowing God at last you become enriched and richer.

For what purpose did life come forth? We believe it is an old question: which came first, the hen or the egg?—a conundrum which has remained unanswered, insoluble. We will pass on what we have learnt in the spiritual schools of wisdom. If this knowledge conflicts with opinions held by the human intellect, well, let it pass.

We say, the hen came first. And we will tell you why the hen came first: because God, the divine intelligence, when creating all things, created them perfect; and the egg results from life and development in the hen, as a seed results from the life process of the flower. Think of creation as the manifestation of a thought sent forth from the mind of God. In the mind of God was conceived an *idea*; God conceived

71

a perfect world. Some consider the story of creation and the birth of Adam into flesh as portrayed in Genesis a childish fable. Yet from the spiritual point of view there are seeds of truth in the old story. We are trying to show you that behind all physical manifestation there is an archetype, a perfect form, a perfect being as originally conceived (and still conceived) in the mind of God.

According to the story there was the perfect type of each life-form in the Garden of Eden, from which perfect types, creation began. If you can think of the rhythm of creation as an out-breathing and an in-breathing 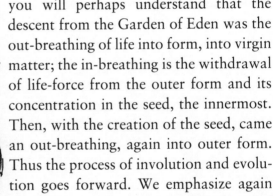 you will perhaps understand that the descent from the Garden of Eden was the out-breathing of life into form, into virgin matter; the in-breathing is the withdrawal of life-force from the outer form and its concentration in the seed, the innermost. Then, with the creation of the seed, came an out-breathing, again into outer form. Thus the process of involution and evolution goes forward. We emphasize again that the perfect type was first conceived in the mind of God, and so took form and life; and the seed was the product of that first divine conception.

So life goes forward without beginning and without end. The wheel is ever spinning. How can the finite mind grasp infinity, or conceive the eternal wheel of life? Truly it is impossible! Yet, while the finite mind falters do you not possess a mind not finite but infinite? Man's spiritual mind is infinite in capacity and scope. Reach beyond limitations to that cosmic consciousness which can be attained even while man dwells in the flesh, if only for one supreme moment. Yet in that moment you will comprehend life in its entirety, see life as a continual in-breathing and out-breathing, as continual involution and evolution. Life will then reveal itself as wholly beautiful, an outpouring of light which knows no end, which always has been and ever shall be.

'But what purpose does life serve?' questions the outer mind. And the inner or spiritual mind replies, 'An ever-unfolding revelation of the beauty of God, and of the meaning of love, of wisdom and of joy'. 'Then what of sickness, suffering, sorrow? Of what use is all this talk of eternity to mortals who suffer and exist only by sweat and labour—what can it mean to the average man?'

Dear ones, hear this: all that you feel is hard, the suffering that you endure, is the road that leads to this inner understanding, this all-pervading love and joy. Suffering is the means of forcing the growth of the seed, and you are the seed which came from the divine. In sending you forth the divine mind conceived you, not as you are now, not as you were ages ago, but as you will become when you have grown from the soil, when you have turned your face away from the shadows to the sunlight, and been caressed by the glory of the light.

Life is mystery, sweet and beautiful, not a drudgery and misery but a joy abounding. . . . And the way to this realization is to lift heart and mind to the sunlight, to respond and grow under the sun as the seed does; to know that all imperfection moves to a definite end, to a continual perfecting. Thus you may become as God conceived and designed you—the perfect son–daughter, made in God's image, yourselves Gods in the making. You are the seed of God. And when you become as God created you, then you, the perfected one, may in turn labour with God for new universes, labour with joy for the glory of creation.

Thus the great wheel ever revolves. When you have thus tasted joy, serenity and all-good, never again will you question the use of life, the wisdom of God; but with all your being you will praise and thank God, and by your praise send forth once more the divine energy and power.

You live on the physical plane confused and bound down by dense matter; but there is a golden ladder from the heart which leads right up to the highest heaven, and angels come and go up and down that ladder to you. Have you ever thought of the watchfulness and the love of your elder brethren who have freed themselves from the bondage in which you now find yourselves? But even the angels cannot interfere with man's karma. Written or impressed within the seed-atom of every one of you is all the karma of the past. The beloved elder brethren or masters, who by self-discipline and slow progress on the evolutionary path have escaped the bondage of earthly matter, have the power to read what lies before every one of you because it is written in the heart, and you yourself have ordained it. To this extent you have freewill. That is to say, whatever life contains is there because you have created it. But we do not want to depress you and make you feel that there is no hope before you. We have come to give a message of more than hope. We have come to give you a message of certainty that you can create beauty and perfection, if you will obey the law of the spirit. The spirit within you, which is *love*, will guide you.

You must not be impatient. You must accept day by day the presentation of your own creation. Accept, accept, accept, and be thankful for the opportunity which life on earth gives to you to stimulate the growth of the divine spirit, deep within you.

You do not yet realize how beautiful is the light. But when the time comes for man to shed the outer clothing, he finds himself in due time in new surroundings and in a new body, and he discovers that all his companions in the new life are clothed in light.

If you have developed clear vision—not just an extension of your earthly vision, but clear vision— you will see that the astral body clothing all the companions who come to you is pulsating with light; countless millions of tiny specks of shining, scintillating light compose the forms of those who have discarded all the lower physical matter. Yet do not think when you reach this stage that this is the end— oh no, you are just beginning! For there is a long way to go, my children, through all the spheres of life. All these states of life, remember, are clothed in matter, and matter even in the astral world can be inhibiting. It is not until the human spirit attains complete mastery over all the planes of matter and reaches the causal plane of life that it is free, free to move as it wills. Such a one has become as perfect as the earthly sojourn can make him. He has become 'man made perfect': this is the goal of every human being.

Do not be disappointed. Do not be dragged down by the mind of earth, by that dense, dark matter in the mind. When you are ready, when you can be trusted, your master will come close to you, and you will be instructed on the inner planes how to go inward and find the true spirit, the light of man, the light of the world.

But do understand that these inner planes are not wispy, cloudy things; to those who inhabit them they are as solid and as real as your physical plane is to you. To us, this desk that we touch* is only real when we touch it with a physical hand, but without the physical hand, there would be no resistance. It is

*White Eagle was indicating the reading desk in front of him as he spoke.

when matter comes up against matter of the same substance that there is resistance. In the world of spirit the matter is finer, but it is still matter, becoming more and more refined as it rises through the planes, until the soul is perfected. Man made perfect! Then he has complete control of matter and he is so spiritually evolved that he only wants to use his power to love, to help, to heal, to lighten the darkness of all his brethren on earth and in all the confines of dense matter.

So, keep on keeping on living the life which your inner voice directs, kindly, lovingly: giving help wherever you can, giving love and sustenance to this great work of illuminating all life. We promise you that as you live faithfully, in obedience to the world of spirit, you will surely, surely and in due time attain to freedom and happiness, a state of perfect life, with so many of your companions and your loved ones with you—because, remember, what you do does not only affect yourself. Your life is like a pebble dropped into a pool of water, creating ripples endlessly. You do not know the end of a word, a thought, an action.

CHAPTER X

THE POWER OF LOVE

Love is the most profound secret of the universe. It is the beginning of life, indeed, it is life itself. Its seed lies within every soul, although many, many incarnations must pass before the majority of souls discover their own secret, the power which lies within their own being. At the present time the earth appears to you to be chaotic, but remember that what appears to be evil is a tester of the human spirit and can quicken the growth of the light within, the light which is love.

You have come from the heavenly state of life as a babe: from a plane of being which is all light, a place pulsating with spiritual light-essence, to which you will all some day return in full consciousness. A babe is largely unconscious of its environment; and the spiritual babe too is not very conscious of its surroundings, or of its own potentialities. In this respect a spiritual babe is like a physical one, utterly dependent upon parents. Its parent, God, enfolds that spiritual babe in love, clothes it in light; and thus clothed in a heavenly garment it is sent forth from its heavenly parent on its long journey to gain knowledge, wisdom, and love. Through gaining love it gains understanding of its life on earth and in the heavens, and the life of the wide universe of which it is a part. The greatest mistake you can make is to think of yourselves as separate from God or from the universe into which you have been born. You are all part of the one whole.

Earth's humanity has always looked to the sun. Every race has left on record its worship of the sun. The ancients knew that the source of all life was the sun, and even beyond the physical life they knew that the sun was a spiritual manifestation of the one universal principle from which all life came. The first principle is Love and love is light. Where there is love, there is light, there is radiance. Where there is no love there is darkness and heaviness. The brothers of the light are the brothers of the Sun, and the brothers of the Sun are brothers of love. All brothers of the light work together as one great master-soul, and this even whilst each individual is separate; even as grains of sand are separate yet together form the seashore—or as drops of water can make an ocean. They serve the grand Architect of the universe as one body, one spirit.

There is a truer and more worthy understanding coming to humanity concerning Christ, the king of the Sun race. You know little of this ancient Sun race, for it has withdrawn from human sight, but these Sun brothers are still around the earth and their influence still inspires and raises the vibrations of humanity; so as you and all humanity look towards the king of love, the king of the Sun race, you enable the light to penetrate the mists. You are working with him and this ancient race to raise the vibrations back again to pure light, to create a world of infinite beauty.

Think ever in terms of light: everything is light. When you think of matter as dark you are increasing its darkness. Think of matter as pulsating light, for this is its true substance when it is held in the mind of Christ, the king of earth's humanity. There is so much to tell about the substance and quality of light, and about those planes beyond the earth which are created out of the substance of light. Without light life would become extinct. Light is life. Yet down below, that light flickers and struggles to keep burning and would die out but for the aspirations, the prayers and the good thoughts of the children of God.

The earth may be in a state of darkness, but the light is coming, even as it came in the ancient days; and pioneers of this great coming are needed. The call has been sent forth to the souls of men and women who have reached a certain stage on their path of evolution; the call to them is to leave all material claims and follow the Master, follow the Son of God.

You will say, 'But we have heard all this before, White Eagle.' But beloved brethren, the message is not clear even yet. More help is coming from the spheres of light so that people will awaken to the power of love, and the scientific implication of this power, for love has power over matter. People are inclined to think that love is synonymous with weakness, but there they are mistaken. Love in the human soul is the greatest power in matter. Love in the human life is magical and can right all wrongs. We are telling you, my brethren, of a power which can transform your life and the life of the whole of humanity. Try it! Demonstrate the power of love for one morning in your home, your shop, your office, wherever your work takes you. Demonstrate—not by telling everyone that you love them, that is not the way—but by holding a steady thought of their God-qualities, by always seeing the good in every condition, striving always for beauty of speech or action or thought. Try it for one half day. Forego the claims of your lower self; hold fast to the source of your inspiration, which is neither your mind nor soul, but your shining spirit, source of all happiness, of all harmony and beauty and light.

Jesus said, *Love one another*. But the Christ, through Jesus, said also: *I am the light of the world.* 'I am.' What did he mean by this? Did he mean that he, the personal Jesus, was the light of the world? This is the interpretation of the orthodox church. But was he not referring to the spark within every human being which you all know as the 'I AM'? Before the world was 'I AM'. I AM the light of the world. I AM the light of life. I AM the light within your own breast. *I and my Father are one*. Man has to learn how to contact that 'I AM' which is within; he has to learn to receive the life-force continually flowing into the human soul, to know the glory of the Father within himself and to manifest that glory. Then he will be filled with light, health, joy and happiness, and will create for himself and for all people a new heaven and a new earth. You and we are pioneers of this new age which is coming through each individual's own effort to reach to understanding of the Master's teaching—the Master who said, *I and my Father are one.*

Yet not by human power alone. Men and women become proud and vain with their own accomplishments, always forgetting that nothing is done without God's love, God's power. Man must never forget that he is a channel, an instrument. Of himself he is powerless; but within him is the light, the Sun, the Son of the divine parents, source of all light. So we see the mystical truth of the holy and blessed trinity—the Father, the Mother, and the Son which is the light within everyone. This it is which must rule the life of the individual and glorify God, and which will build 'a new heaven and a new earth'.

In your lodge may there spread the radiance of love.* Do not let the arrogant earthly mind enter into

*These words, spoken to members of White Eagle's own community or Lodge (the word 'lodge' comes from his ownNative American culture) seem to us to be applicable to everyone, as a reflection on their own inner temple or lodge of the spirit.

it. Preserve here, by the grace of God, the spirit of brotherly love, the spirit of kindness and humility; the spirit of comradeship and companionship. Let this small lodge radiate the power of the Son. From this small beginning may the whole world ring with the glory and the power of God. May heaven come to earth!—not by our growing sanctimonious or proud, thinking that we are unlike other people, but being comrades to all and unwearied in our service to our brother and in our attunement to God, and by using the creative power of the Son which God has placed in our hearts. Set aside a time each day for quiet—either wandering in the green places, the woods or the country lanes, or, if this is not possible, by going into the green and sunlit countryside within your own heart. Seek the place of eternal silence, and in that silence you will receive your food, the bread and the wine of life. For any man or woman who has truly held such a communion, there will be no more death. When your physical experience is finished, you will know no death. You may shed your overcoat of flesh as does a butterfly released from its chrysalis. Then you will return into the freedom of heaven in full consciousness of the power of God in you—your birthright. The outer life will become a reflection of that joyousness which irradiates your innermost being in the silence.

CHAPTER XI

BEAUTIFUL ROAD HOME

We would describe for you a mystery, the reunion of the holy family. That is, of the Father (divine will and energy), the Mother (divine love and wisdom) and the Child, the Son of God. The Son is, shall we say, the light which lighteth the way for every man and woman. It is that light within you which guides you from the time you are given birth, conceived by the divine will and energy and the divine love and wisdom.

Thus the light is born and the light is the Son; but the light becomes obscured as it descends. Clothed in denser and denser matter, it becomes dimmed; but as the light begins to overcome the darkness, the path of return to divine will and energy and divine love and wisdom is made clearer. The soul commences its return on an upward arc, eventually to become reunited with its source. It leaves that source at the beginning of its being, a babe, unaware and unconscious of its inner powers. It returns to complete reunion with its source, having learned through its experiences in the darkness that it is a child of God. Then it becomes at one with the Father–Mother—the two first principles of life—and the light or the Son of God being thus reunited within the holy family, completes the perfect trinity of life.

You have chosen to read our words because you have begun to be aware of your inner light. You are no longer wholly imprisoned in the lower mind or in the bonds of materiality. You are like the Israelites in the story of the liberation from the bondage of Egypt: Is-ra-elites, 'Ra' meaning light. You are sons and daughters following the light of God. When we are told that the children of Israel were led out of the house of bondage, they stand as symbolic of those souls which are evolving upwards— souls which once descended without consciousness down and down into the depths. Awakened by the words, the teachings of the initiate, they are led out of captivity; but they have yet to enter the land flowing with milk and honey which they are promised. They are still in the wilderness.

Many people wander in such a wilderness today. Many people have been awakened to the possibility of a life which does not need a physical body, a life which goes on after death. Many souls, having seen a vision of the spirit life, are very anxious to keep in touch with the spirit world and to develop psychic powers. But there is a better way of holding true and perfect communion with the world of spirit, which has always been taught to those people who have proved themselves ready for such knowledge. For when the soul has discerned the true light, when the light of the gentle Christ is illumining its path, the soul will find that with true spiritual at-one-ment and communion, roses will bloom even in the wilderness.

We could say more about that wondrous flower, the rose. Shall we call it the queen of flowers—the symbolic flower into which all souls will be absorbed? For the spiritual rose represents the supreme Christ love, the perfect love; and the aspirant will find on the true path roses instead of barren rocks, if he will only be guided by those who follow the true and correct path of unfoldment.

Although the mind can be depicted by those barren rocks, the higher mind is that part of your mind which must be developed by the experience of 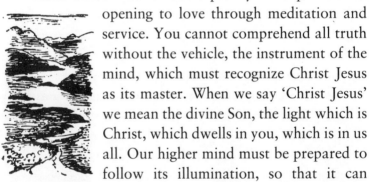 opening to love through meditation and service. You cannot comprehend all truth without the vehicle, the instrument of the mind, which must recognize Christ Jesus as its master. When we say 'Christ Jesus' we mean the divine Son, the light which is Christ, which dwells in you, which is in us all. Our higher mind must be prepared to follow its illumination, so that it can comprehend divine truth, clothe it, express it in words and so convey it to others. While it is true that divine truth may be conveyed through light and love, it is also necessary to be able to clothe it through the higher mind in words.

We come back again to the starting point. We see in the wondrous story of the crucifixion of the body—

of the lower mind—the passing away of worldly things, the flight from the land of Egypt. We see the light which is the higher mind, developed so that full consciousness of cosmic truth wakes within. We see the evolved man and woman returning again to the divine source, taking with them that beautiful rose which they have gathered in the wilderness of emotions, the wilderness of the mind, and even the wilderness of materialism. The individual having gathered the rose, it blooms upon his or her heart, the symbol of the Christ love. This is the meaning of the saying which many of you know, 'May the rose bloom upon your cross'—the rose of the Christ essence, true brotherliness, divine truth.

This is the journey of the soul, my brethren. Even though you are in the wilderness now, you will be led into the Promised Land. We all move forward up the path to the heights upon which is enthroned God. You remember the story of Moses going up the mountain, seeing the vision of God and telling the people? This is for you and for us. We also shall climb that mountain to the golden heights. We shall take with us upon our hearts the fragrant, perfect rose of the Christ-life. May you absorb this blessing from the heights and go your way rejoicing.

*

A wonderful star is now above your heads here, the blazing Star of the Brotherhood of the ages, the symbol of the Son, the Christos. And the rays of light from this star are now pouring into your hearts, awakening you to the glorious future which is before you. But you have to work towards it. You cannot be carried. You have got to work and work and serve your brother man and all creation. Love mother earth, treat her kindly. Love your body, the temple of your spirit. Don't knock it about, over-feed it or put impure food into it. Take in pure simple food, and plenty of the waters from the mountains and the skies. Live with peace in your heart towards life, towards all people. Love one another—that is all. And you will be saviours, all of you will be saviours. However insignificant you think yourself to be you can still be a saviour and a giver of happiness to others.

God is infinite, illimitable, God is all-enfolding, God is within you and around you and above you and beneath you; you live and move and have your being in God. And the purpose of human life, the purpose of all your experiences, your striving, your sorrow, your joys, is to mould your spirit and soul into a perfect son–daughter of God, man–woman made perfect. This lies before every one of you. If human-kind remains loyal and true to the divine light within the heart; and if you, if everyone who hears and reads our words, awakens to their responsibility of helping their fellow man and woman to understand the purpose of life, and that within them is this divine light which will liberate them from the bondage of evil and darkness and conflict, then the earth planet will enter a new golden age, when the Son of God, the great Sun in the heavens, will manifest in glory on the earth; all tears will be washed away, people will live together in harmony, in peace and joy.

And after this, what then? Humanity by its own striving and development of the power of the Sun in the heart will change physical matter. You have the demonstration of this in the resurrection of Jesus, the Christ; and he said to you, 'What I do shall you do also.' With this growth of the Christ light in physical matter there will be a purification and a beautifying of all life, until this planet, this dark star, will become a brilliant Sun—not tomorrow, but in the eternal life.

This, my children, is the meaning of the resurrection—the growth of life, the development of the golden seed of life planted in man in the beginning of time.

God bless you; God bless you, everyone. Peace be with you, for God is love.

CHAPTER XII

EPILOGUE: THE GOLDEN CITY

*These words of White Eagle's, given at the beginning
of the Easter festival, seem to form a 'crown' for what
has gone before.*

All souls desire truth, knowledge and wisdom. All
souls desire happiness and joy; all souls yearn in their
innermost for God.

At the spring equinox there pours forth upon the
earth a baptism of power and spiritual sunlight, of
life-force, which stimulates the life within mother
earth, causing growth to take place from her womb.
But there is also a spiritual power which floods
mankind. While many do not understand this, they
still register a certain joy from hearing the birds sing
and seeing the flowers blossom and from all the
beauty of spring. They want to cry out, 'Oh, it is good
to be alive! What a lovely spring day!'

We would like you to come one step further; not
only to be happy because of the coming spring, but
to realize its deeper meaning—realize that with the
spring equinox there is descending this blazing light,

a glorious power and a spiritual inspiration. This should help you to raise your consciousness to heavenly planes, to grow in understanding of that Golden City referred to in the words of St John.

Where is this City to be found? Is it something external? Or is it something within man himself? It is both, my friends. But first it is deep within you all. Yet what is *within* has eventually to become externalized, or expressed *outside* man. Do you know that when a soul passes away after death, the condition in which it finds itself reflects the thoughts and feelings with which it habitually lived while in the physical body? Its surroundings are those of its own thought, its own aspiration, externalized. With whatever a man or woman fills his or her thoughts on earth, they will, to begin with, surround themselves in the life beyond. Even your homes will be externalized—libraries, much loved pictures, beloved gardens, favourite places of holiday—all that has delighted the soul will be exactly what it will find when it lives in the world of spirit.

Man grows spiritually as a child grows to adulthood and afterwards he continues to grow from man's estate to angelic estate. There is a passage in the bible which says that the human soul, if it overcome all things, shall become God's son–daughter and angel. There are planes of life undreamed of by you who are imprisoned in earthiness. But this does not mean that comprehension of these glories in the heavens cannot be realized whilst still living in the physical body. When a soul grows in awareness of God through aspiration, meditation, prayer and love, that soul is being prepared for initiation into the Golden City.

You read that this City has twelve foundations ... the twelve foundations being the twelve qualities of the soul, the essential qualities upon which to build 'Jerusalem' within the soul. The twelve gates referred to, and the twelve tribes, we interpret to mean the twelve perfected types of men and women, the twelve perfect signs of the zodiac. Three gates each were at the North, the South, the East and West; are these not earth, air, fire and water, the elements with which man builds the perfect City?

There is another important realization—John says there is no sea in the new heaven and the new earth. We offer you the thought that this means that there is no division, no dividing line between earth and heaven; that in this new City, this new state of life to which man is advancing, there will be an interpenetration of all life, both heavenly and earthly. We see in this the perfect balance expressed by the symbol of the six-pointed star. All seers know that heaven and earth interpenetrate, and this interpenetration must be manifested in human form. When the seer sees a vision, when in his higher faculties he walks in the golden streets of the Golden City, he knows that it does not incapacitate him for his daily work, but gives a more perfect body and mind, a more perfect spiritual life, lived both on earth and in heaven.

The division which the sea symbolizes has eventually to be done away with. It will be overcome and there will be a perfect interpenetration of the heavenly and the earthly life. This heavenly City is paralleled by the Chinese teaching of the Golden Flower. The Golden City and the Golden Flower stand for the centre of the heart, that innermost state, which all can reach, of divine illumination, which comes to man through aspiration and true meditation. The new Jerusalem is built upon the foundation of the twelve virtues of life. When you read that the angel takes the measuring rod of 144 cubits, and finds the perfect cube, the perfect square, this means that the soul of man perfected is represented by the perfect square; and the number of the perfect man–woman is nine ... represented by the digits of the number 144 added together.

The new Jerusalem is the soul made perfect, or man–woman made perfect. This, my friends, is the goal of all seekers after truth. Do not think, either, that it is just a condition which awaits you thousands upon thousands of years hence. You can begin to understand this perfect life now.

Is this not a vision worth striving after, worth living for? We assure you that all the confusion, all the sickness of body and mind, all the inconvenience and the sorrows and the separation of this present time on earth, all fall away when this true vision is established in the heart, in the mind, in the soul of every individual. Beloved brethren, when Jesus wept over Jerusalem, he wept not just over the city in Israel, but for the suffering and sorrowful soul of humanity.

So, we leave you with thanksgiving to our Creator. May divine peace enfold you all; may divine truth be uncovered, deep though it may lie within your consciousness. May you see this vision of the new Jerusalem that lies within your innermost being; and then may your vision be externalized on earth, on all the planes of life.